Little Red Hen is Cooking

Based on a Folktale
by Rob Arego

Little Red Hen is cooking.
"What are you cooking?" asks Cat.

2

"Soup," says Hen. "Do you like soup?"
"Yes, I do," says Cat.

"Help me cook the soup," says Hen.
"No," says Cat.

4

"What are you cooking?" asks Cat.

"Cookies," says Hen. "Do you like cookies?"
"Yes, I do!" says Cat.

"Help me make the cookies," says Hen.
"No," says Cat.

"What are you eating and drinking?" Cat asks.

"My food," says Hen. "It's good."

"May I have soup and cookies, please?" asks Cat.

"I'm sorry," says Hen.
"You didn't help me cook.
You can't help me eat!"

11

Facts About Food

Eggs come from chickens.

Milk comes from cows.

12

Oranges and orange juice
come from trees.

Mmm! Good!

Bananas
come from
trees, too.

13

Fun with Food

Do you eat it or drink it?

orange juice   eggs   milk   cookies

Eat	Drink
eggs	

Look at the letters. Write the food word.

nabnaa

banana

geg

_____

upos

_____

lkmi

_____

15

Glossary

cat

help

hen